10/12

D1379575

DEER HUNTING

BY BLAKE POUND

BELLWETHER MEDIA · MINNEAPOLIS, MN

Jump into the cockpit and take flight with Pilot books. Your journey will take you on high-energy adventures as you learn about all that is wild, weird, fascinating, and fun!

This edition first published in 2013 by Bellwether Media, Inc.

No part of this publication may be reproduced in whole or in part without written permission of the publisher. For information regarding permission, write to Bellwether Media, Inc., Attention: Permissions Department, 5357 Penn Avenue South, Minneapolis, MN 55419.

Library of Congress Cataloging-in-Publication Data

Pound, Blake.
 Deer hunting / by Blake Pound.
   p. cm. – (Pilot books: outdoor adventures)
 Includes bibliographical references and index.
 Summary: "Engaging images accompany information about deer hunting. The combination of high-interest subject matter and narrative text is intended for students in grades 3 through 7"–Provided by publisher.
 ISBN 978-1-60014-796-8 (hardcover : alk. paper)
 1. Deer hunting–Juvenile literature. I. Title.
 SK301.P69 2013
 799.2'765–dc23
                     2012000960

Printed in the United States of America, North Mankato, MN.

TABLE OF CONTENTS

ON THE HUNT

A cool fall breeze blows as two hunters walk through a forest. The trees are bare, and leaves cover the ground. One of the hunters spots a **buck** on top of a hill. Its antlers have six **points**. The hunter moves to a clear line of sight. He raises his rifle and aims carefully through the **scope**.

Just then, the other hunter takes a small step forward. A twig snaps under his foot. The startled deer runs deeper into the woods. The hunter lowers his rifle. He may have to wait hours for another chance at a buck.

Deer hunting is a popular fall sport. Every year, millions of hunters head to the woods in search of a trophy buck. The most serious hunters **scout** before deer hunting season. They search for the best **deer trails** in the area.

A Helping Hand

Some people work as professional hunting guides. They direct hunters to deer trails and places where deer like to drink, rest, and graze.

DEER HUNTED IN THE UNITED STATES

Species	Location
White-tailed deer	Eastern, Central, and Northwestern United States
Mule deer	Western United States
Elk	Northwestern United States
Moose	Northern United States
Caribou	Alaska

Deer hunting is usually a group activity, but hunters must stay silent. They must also keep their distance when following a deer. Deer have great hearing and an excellent sense of smell. They are very afraid of humans. If they hear footsteps or smell a human, they will run away at speeds up to 30 miles (48 kilometers) per hour.

deer stand

People hunt deer in a couple different ways. Many hunters use deer stands. These are small platforms that allow hunters to watch for deer from above. It is important to keep very still in this type of deer hunting.

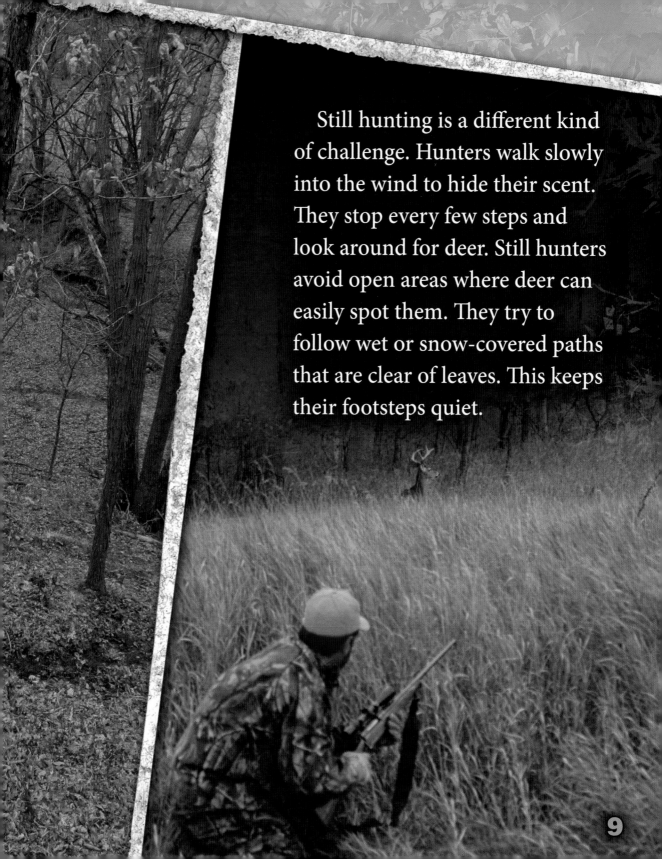

Still hunting is a different kind of challenge. Hunters walk slowly into the wind to hide their scent. They stop every few steps and look around for deer. Still hunters avoid open areas where deer can easily spot them. They try to follow wet or snow-covered paths that are clear of leaves. This keeps their footsteps quiet.

DEER HUNTING EQUIPMENT

Deer hunting requires a lot of gear. Every deer hunter needs a rifle with a long **barrel**. Tiny grooves in the barrel help bullets travel straight. Scopes help hunters aim. They have **crosshairs** to line up shots. The best scopes can help hunters bring down deer from hundreds of feet away.

Thick clothing keeps hunters warm in cool fall weather. **Camouflage** helps them blend in with surrounding leaves and branches. Most states require hunters to wear a certain amount of **blaze orange**. This keeps them visible to other hunters. Heavy rubber boots keep feet dry and trap odors. This makes it harder for deer to pick up a hunter's scent.

Straight to the Point

Some hunters use bows and arrows to hunt deer. Bow hunters need strength to draw the bowstring back. Practice helps them release arrows straight at targets.

Hunters have many methods of attracting deer. Some use sound. **Deer calls** can sound like a crying fawn or a grunting buck. If hunters have antlers, they can rattle them together to make the sound of two bucks fighting. This will often attract other bucks that want to join the battle.

Deer hunters also use food to lure deer into the open. Deer especially love acorns and **persimmons**. They are also attracted by the scent of deer urine. Hunters often scatter deer urine in a clearing. They also soak rags in the urine and drag them along the ground to create a scent trail.

Deer **decoys** can also be used to draw deer out of their hiding places. Hunters place decoys in an open area or near a deer stand. Some decoys have small, quiet motors that gently flick their tails. This signals to other deer that the area is safe.

PLANNING AND PREPARATION

Deer hunters must plan ahead. All hunters must have a **license** before they hunt. Many states require hunters to pass a gun safety class before they can get a license. Every state has its own hunting laws and hunting season. Hunters must stay clear of **wildlife reserves** and other areas where hunting is not permitted.

Many hunters return to woods where they have had success. Any new hunting grounds should be scouted for deer and deer trails. Before the hunt, weapons and gear should be cleaned and packed for easy transport.

DEER HUNTING CHECKLIST

- Warm camouflage and blaze orange clothing
- Weapon and ammunition
- Comfortable rubber boots
- Decoys, deer calls, or bait
- Energizing snacks and drinks
- Flashlight
- Maps and compass
- License
- Binoculars

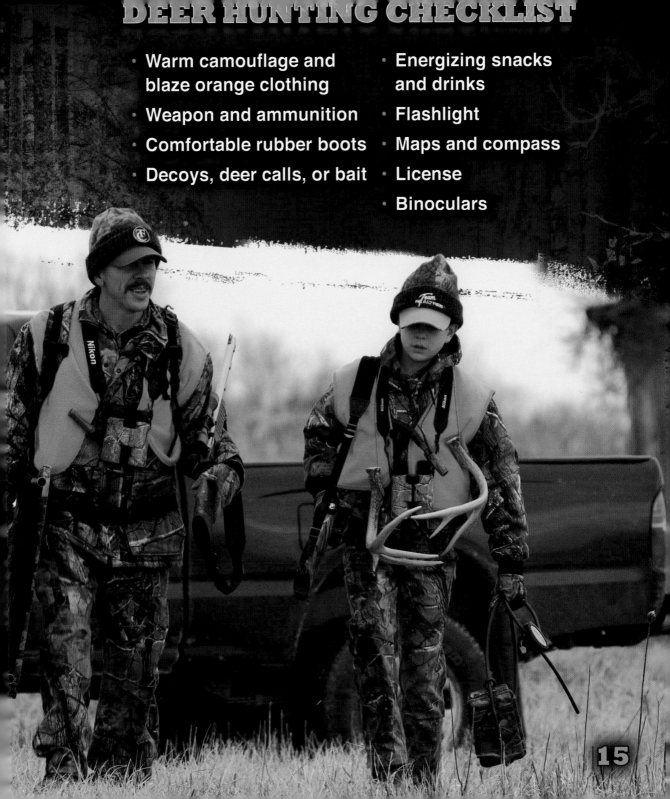

Responsible deer hunters follow a **code of conduct**. If they see another hunter nearby, they move to a different area. They never shoot at a deer that another hunter is tracking. Hunters know to only fire their weapons if they have a clear shot.

If they want to hunt on private land, hunters need to get permission from the landowner. Care must be taken to not damage crops, fences, trees, or buildings. Hunters should never shoot across footpaths, toward buildings, or anywhere else people might be. When hunters have finished for the day, they should take all of their gear and trash with them.

Friendly Farmers

Deer often eat crops and damage farm fields. Many farmers are happy to allow deer hunters access to their lands.

Deer hunters in the same group need to practice safety. They should never point their rifles at one another. If one hunter is aiming for a shot, the others should point their rifles toward the ground. When not hunting, guns should be unloaded and locked away.

It is important that hunters care for and **preserve** the land. All deer hunters should have an interest in making deer hunting possible for future generations. Hunters should only take the number of deer allowed by law and respect the environment at all times. If hunters follow the law and respect one another, deer hunting can be enjoyed for many years to come.

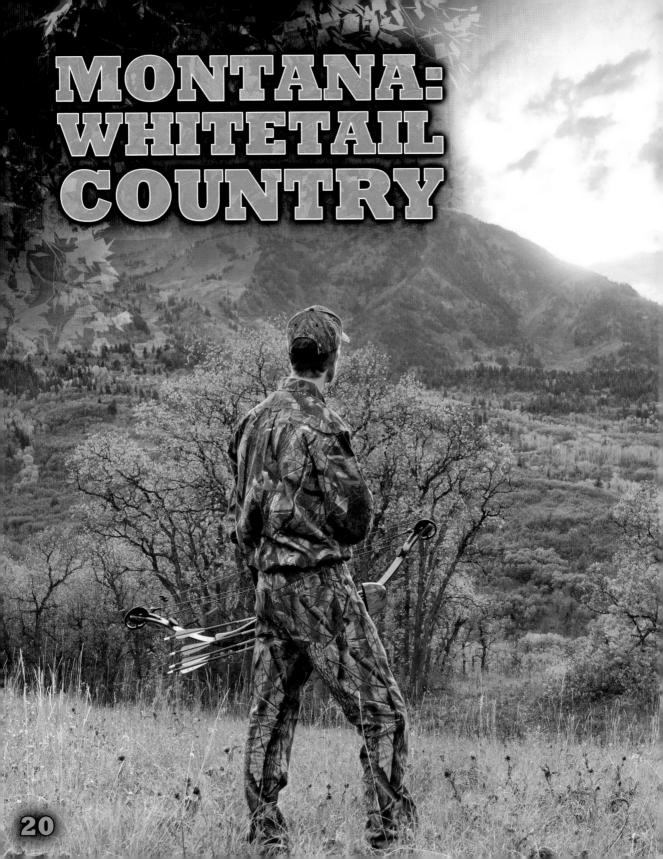

MONTANA: WHITETAIL COUNTRY

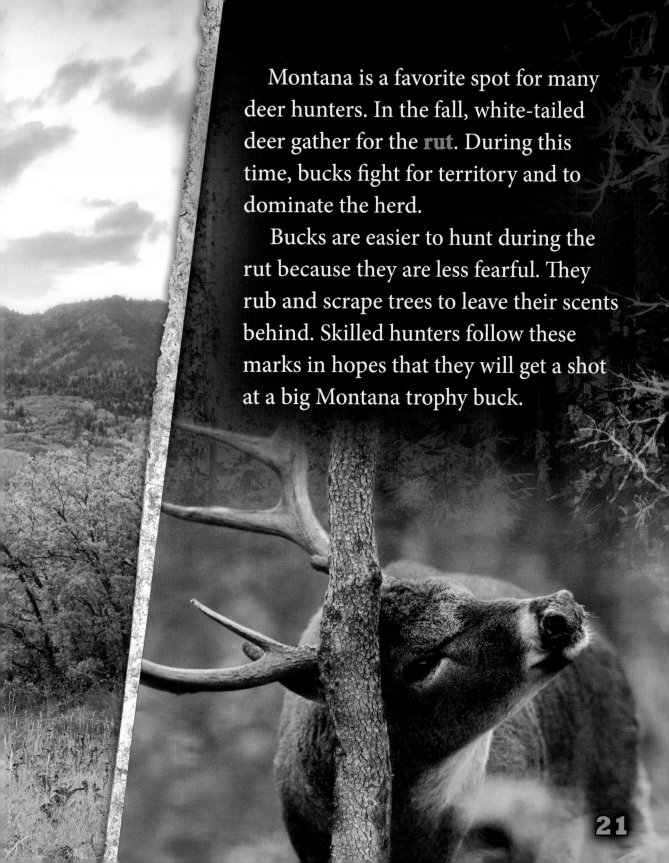

Montana is a favorite spot for many deer hunters. In the fall, white-tailed deer gather for the **rut**. During this time, bucks fight for territory and to dominate the herd.

Bucks are easier to hunt during the rut because they are less fearful. They rub and scrape trees to leave their scents behind. Skilled hunters follow these marks in hopes that they will get a shot at a big Montana trophy buck.

GLOSSARY

barrel—the long, straight part of a gun; bullets travel through the barrel and out of the gun.

blaze orange—the color most hunters are required to wear for safety; deer cannot see blaze orange.

buck—a male deer

camouflage—clothing with coloring and patterns that blend in with the surroundings

code of conduct—a set of rules that establishes how a person should behave; hunters follow a code of conduct to respect one another and the land.

crosshairs—thin lines that form a cross in a scope; crosshairs help hunters aim their weapons.

decoys—life-like models of deer; decoys are used to attract deer.

deer calls—noisemakers that mimic the sounds deer make; deer calls are used to attract deer.

deer trails—paths that deer often travel

license—a document that gives legal permission to do an activity

persimmons—small orange fruits that grow on trees and look like tomatoes

points—the small, sharp tips that grow on the ends of a buck's antlers; older bucks have more points.

preserve—to keep protected

rut—the season when deer mate

scope—a small telescope that allows a hunter to see long distances and aim his or her weapon

scout—to explore an area to learn more about it

wildlife reserves—areas that protect deer and other animals; hunting is not permitted in most reserves.

TO LEARN MORE

At the Library

Adamson, Thomas K. *Deer Hunting*. Mankato, Minn.:
Capstone Press, 2011.

MacRae, Sloan. *Deer Hunting*. New York, N.Y.:
PowerKids Press, 2011.

Weber, Susan Bartlett. *Opening Day*. Gardiner, Maine:
Tilbury House, 2007.

On the Web

Learning more about deer hunting
is as easy as 1, 2, 3.

1. Go to www.factsurfer.com.

2. Enter "deer hunting" into the search box.

3. Click the "Surf" button and you will see a list
of related Web sites.

With factsurfer.com, finding more information
is just a click away.

INDEX